Usborne

First Sticker Book

Sports Day

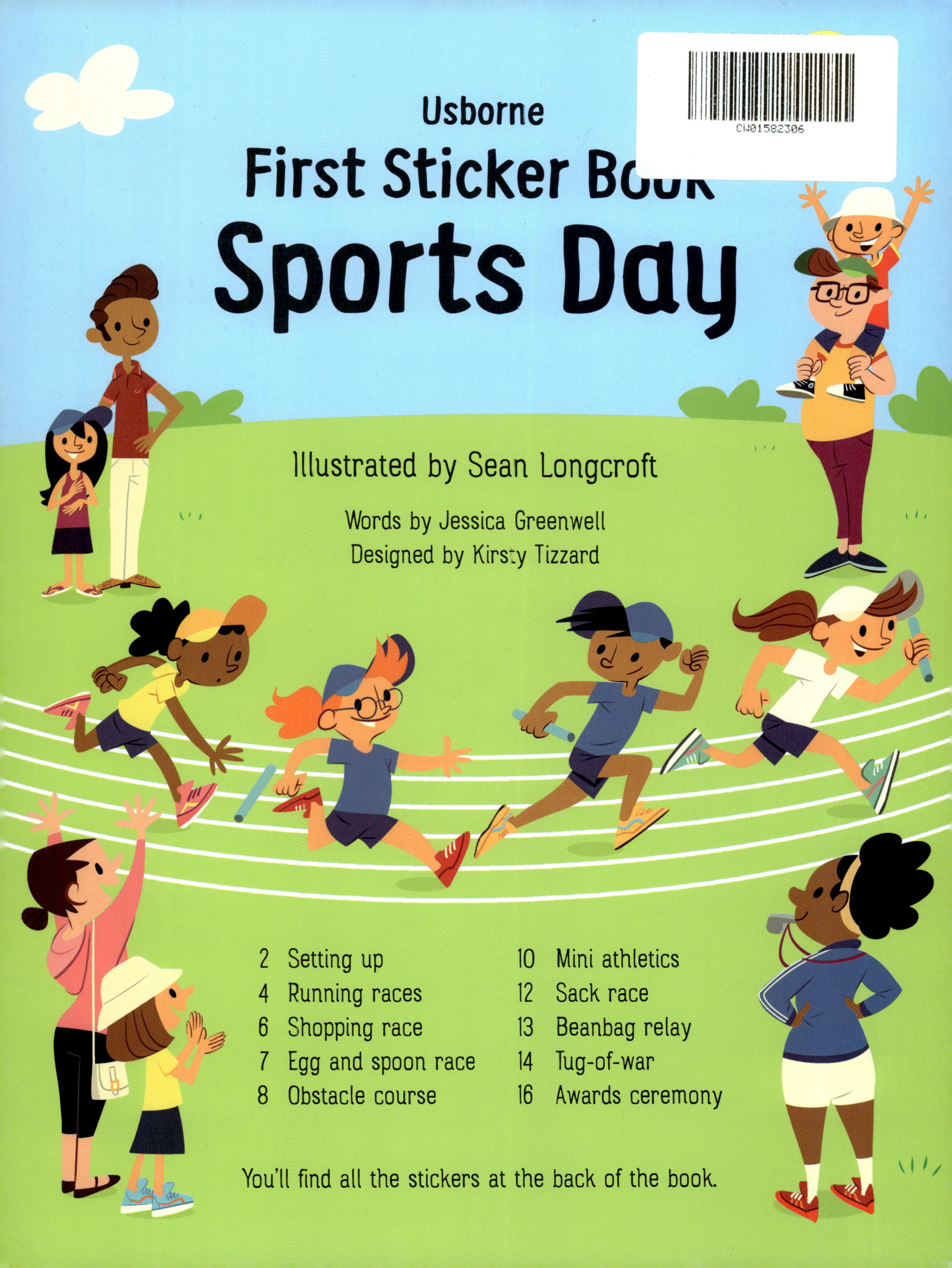

Illustrated by Sean Longcroft

Words by Jessica Greenwell

Designed by Kirsty Tizzard

You'll find all the stickers at the back of the book.

Setting up

It's Sports Day at this school and there's lots of excitement as the teachers and children get ready for the games to begin. Use the stickers to finish the scene.

RACES
Drinks

Running races

And they're off! The running races are in full swing. Stick on lots more speedy sprinters and choose who will win first place in each race.

Shopping race

In this game, children run to collect toy food in their shopping baskets. The first person to fill their basket will be the winner! Put all the children in the race.

Egg and spoon race

It can be tricky to balance an egg and run at the same time in this fun race. Stick on some more children and some cheering spectators.

Obstacle course

With tunnels, balance beams, bridges and ladders, this course is lots of fun. Stick on all the children crawling through or scrambling over each obstacle.

Mini athletics

In the school hall there's an athletics competition. Stick on all the children taking part in the long jump, the foam javelin and the beanbag shot put.

Team Sports at School
FOAM JAVELIN
BEANBAGS

Sack race

The children hop and jump to the finish line in their sacks. Put them all on the track and add some more grown-ups watching the race.

Beanbag relay

In a relay race the children compete in teams. Stick them all on, carefully balancing their beanbags on their heads and trying not to drop them.

Tug-of-war

This exciting game is a test of strength and team work. Add all the stickers to make a tug-of-war for the children, and another for the grown-ups.

Awards ceremony

It's time for the children to receive their awards. There's a medal for everyone and a shield for the winning team. Add all the stickers to the picture.

Setting up pages 2–3

Running races pages 4–5

Children racing

Water bottles

Children warming up

Spectators

Teachers

Shopping race page 6

Egg and spoon race page 7

Obstacle course pages 8-9

First aid kit

Balance beam

Spectators

Rope ladders

Children cheering

Flags

Bridges

Tunnels

Mini athletics pages 10–11

Sack race page 12

Beanbag relay page 13

Tug-of-war pages 14–15

Awards ceremony page 16

You can use these stickers wherever you like.